T0071001

Vaughan Williams for Choirs 1

JOHN LEAVITT

10 sacred pieces compiled and arranged for accompanied mixed voices

MUSIC DEPARTMENT

OXFORD
UNIVERSITY PRESS

OXFORD
UNIVERSITY PRESS

Great Clarendon Street, Oxford OX2 6DP,
United Kingdom

Oxford University Press is a department of the University of Oxford.
It furthers the University's objective of excellence in research, scholarship,
and education by publishing worldwide. Oxford is a registered trade mark of
Oxford University Press in the UK and in certain other countries

This collection © Oxford University Press 2020

John Leavitt has asserted his right under the Copyright, Designs
and Patents Act, 1988, to be identified as the Editor of this anthology

First published 2020

Impression: 1

All rights reserved. No part of this publication may be reproduced,
stored in a retrieval system, or transmitted, in any form or by any means,
without the prior permission in writing of Oxford University Press

Permission to perform the works in this anthology in public
(except in the course of divine worship) should normally be obtained
from the Performing Right Society Ltd (PRS) at www.prsformusic.com
or a local performing right licensing organization, unless the owner or the
occupier of the premises being used already holds a licence from such an
organization. Likewise, permission to make and exploit a recording must
be obtained in advance from the Mechanical-Copyright Protection
Society Ltd (MCPS) at www.prsformusic.com or a local mechanical
copyright licensing organization

Enquiries concerning reproduction outside the scope of the above should be
directed to the Music Rights Department, Oxford University Press, at
music.permissions.uk@oup.com or at the address above

ISBN 978-0-19-353210-6

Music origination by Andrew Jones
Text origination by Michael Durnin
Printed in Great Britain on acid-free paper by
Halstan & Co. Ltd, Amersham, Bucks.

Contents

Preface	iv
Notes on the pieces	v
The blessed son of God	8
No sad thought his soul affright	14
A Song of Thanksgiving	18
This is the truth	30
O taste and see	37
God rest you merry, gentlemen	40
O how amiable	47
He that is down need fear no fall	54
At the name of Jesus	59
Let us now praise famous men	72
'He that is down need fear no fall' clarinet part	76

Preface

Welcome to this collection of new arrangements of short choral pieces by one of the finest British composers of the twentieth century. Born in 1872 in Gloucestershire, Ralph Vaughan Williams attended the Royal College of Music and read history and music at Trinity College, Cambridge. He studied composition with C. Hubert H. Parry and Charles Villiers Stanford, and received further tuition overseas from Max Bruch and Maurice Ravel. After a distinguished career, producing a particularly wide-ranging catalogue of works, Vaughan Williams died on 26 August 1958. His ashes were interred at Westminster Abbey.

Vaughan Williams's various musical activities—from choir master, editor, and folk-song collector to composer and conductor—greatly enhanced British musical life; but they also contributed to a mistaken view that his original composition was in some way parochial, designed for domestic consumption. He believed in the value of music education, and wrote pieces for amateurs and service music for the church; but he also displayed great sensitivity to the twentieth-century human condition, projecting a message of peace and reconciliation in works such as *Dona Nobis Pacem* (1936). Moreover, he wrote works of great artistic integrity and imagination that have stood the test of time, not least for choirs, and for all levels of music making.

Vaughan Williams was inspired by great literature and by a lifelong belief that the voice 'can be made the medium of the best and deepest human emotion' (*Vaughan Williams on Music*, ed. D. Manning, Oxford, 2007). Made up of two volumes and organized into sacred and secular works, the current collection is designed to introduce new generations of choral conductors and choirs to Vaughan Williams, sharing his music's variety and timeless quality. There is a mix of familiar and unfamiliar titles. A second aim was to make the pieces, where necessary, match today's scoring and performance needs, improving accessibility and extending their usefulness in a way that would have appealed to Vaughan Williams. At one extreme the arrangements have new piano parts for unaccompanied sections, for example, to lend support, or contain small judicious cuts. Others are arranged in a friendlier key (taking into account the range, also), or for SATB choir from a unison or treble-voice original—the subject matter and content lending itself equally well to adults. At the other end, pieces were selected for their ongoing appeal and suitability, requiring no more than light editorial amendments. In all cases, the harmony, words, and dynamics are unaltered, and my aim has been to respect the integrity and spirit of the original work.

The following commentary, on individual pieces, specifies the changes, sources, and possible uses in performance.

Finally, I wish to record my thanks to Oxford University Press for assisting my research and allowing access to its extensive catalogue, and to The Vaughan Williams Charitable Trust for its kind support.

John Leavitt
2019

Notes on the pieces

The blessed son of God from the cantata 'Hodie'

Source: 'Two Chorals', OUP, 1954
Suggested programming: Christmas (concert or church)

A piano accompaniment has been added which conforms to the original harmonic structure of the choral parts. A short introduction has been added, and the first verse is now scored for tutti sopranos or an optional solo. The piano pedalling should be modest and appropriate to the harmonic changes.

No sad thought his soul affright from the cantata 'Hodie'

Source: 'Two Chorals', OUP, 1954
Suggested programming: Christmas (concert or church)

This piece has been lowered by a semitone to C major, making it easier to read, and with a more accessible tenor part. A piano accompaniment has been added which conforms to the original harmonic structure of the choral parts. It was common for composers of music from this period to extend the dynamic range. In this case the markings ***pp*** and ***ppp*** may need to be adjusted, depending on the size and capability of the ensemble, to achieve a hushed, intimate sound. The piano pedalling should be modest and appropriate to the harmonic changes.

A Song of Thanksgiving

Source: 'A Song of Thanksgiving', OUP, 1945
Suggested programming: Concert or church (Thanksgiving, general praise)

This large work has been edited down to the first 125 bars/measures to make it a suitable length for a general anthem of thanksgiving. There is an optional shortened ending after bar/measure 116. The piano pedalling should be modest and appropriate to the harmonic changes.

This is the truth

Source: 'This is the truth', OUP, 1954
Suggested programming: Christmas (concert or church)

This unison arrangement has been reworked into a setting for SATB chorus with an optional soloist. The harmony of the SATB parts conforms to the original harmony of the piano part. Some mild figuration has also been added occasionally to the piano part in the first section of the piece. The piano pedalling should be used sparingly so as not to blur the musical lines.

O taste and see, a setting of Psalm 34: 8

Source: 'O Taste and See', OUP, 1953
Suggested programming: Church (Wedding, All Saints, 23rd Sunday after Pentecost)

This piece was written and first performed for the coronation of Queen Elizabeth II. The only change applies to the *colla parte* piano part from bar/measure 13 to the end, where it is indicated that the piano may optionally double the voices, either for support or colour. If the piano is used, it should be played *secco*.

God rest you merry, gentlemen

Source: 'God Rest You Merry', for SA chorus and piano, OUP, 1954, renewed in the USA, 1982
Suggested programming: Christmas (concert or church)

This piece was originally arranged by Vaughan Williams for SA voices and piano. Here, it has been rearranged for SATB voices and piano. The new vocal parts conform to the original harmonic structure. The piano pedalling for this arrangement should be used sparingly so as not to blur the musical lines.

O how amiable

Source: 'O how amiable', OUP, 1940
Suggested programming: Church dedication, or other festivals

Some slight adjustments have been made to the organ part to adapt it for the piano, including octave displacements, added octaves, and deleted octaves. Vaughan Williams marked much of the original organ part with slurs, which suggests a *legato* feel. If the piano pedal is used at all, then it should be used sparingly and for colour.

He that is down need fear no fall

Source: 'He that is down need fear no fall', Oxford Choral Songs (unison and piano), OUP, 1950
Suggested programming: Concert or funeral

This unison anthem has been reworked into a setting for SATB choir with an optional soloist. The harmony of the SATB parts conforms to the original harmony of the piano part. If the piano pedal is used at all, then it should be used sparingly, without blurring the musical lines.

At the name of Jesus

Source: 'At the name of Jesus', OUP, 1927, renewed in the USA, 1955
Suggested programming: Church (Ascension, Feast of Christ the King, Fourth Sunday in Advent)

Some small changes have been made in the dispensation of the forces in the choral parts. In the original, all voices sing verses 1 and 2 in unison; in this arrangement the upper voices sing verse 1 and the lower voices sing verse 2. In verses 4 and 6 some sopranos sing the descant and the remaining SATB choir sing in unison. A light optional piano accompaniment has been added in verse 5. Verse 7 has been arranged for SATB instead of unison voices. In the final phrase the sopranos sing a short descant for a stronger ending, with the tenors and sopranos singing in a higher tessitura. The harmony of any changes to the choral parts conforms to the original harmonic structure. The piano pedal should be used sparingly and avoid blurring the musical lines. It should not be used at all in the section with the staccato left-hand bass (verse 5).

Let us now praise famous men

Source: 'The New Church Anthem Book', OUP, 1992
Suggested programming: Church (All Saints)

This unison anthem has been revoiced for SATB choir. The harmony of the SATB parts conforms to the original harmony of the piano part. The pedal should not be used for most of this piece.

The blessed son of God

from the cantata 'Hodie'

Miles Coverdale (1487–1569),
after Martin Luther

RALPH VAUGHAN WILLIAMS (1872–1958)
piano arranged by John Leavitt

Duration: *c.*2 mins

© Oxford University Press 1954 and 2020

12
our poor flesh and our poor blood Was clothed that ev - er -
18
-last - ing good. Ky - ri - e - lei - son.
Lord have mer - cy.
TUTTI
24
p dolce
S.
The Lord Christ Je - su, God's son dear, Was a guest and a
A.
The Lord Christ Je - su, God's son dear, Was a guest and a
T.
The Lord Christ Je - su, God's son dear, Was a guest and a
B.
The Lord Christ Je - su, God's son dear, Was a guest and a

30
strang - er here; Us for to bring from mi - se - ry, That
strang - er here; Us for to bring from mi - se - ry, That
strang - er here; Us for to bring from mi - se - ry, That
strang - er here; Us for to bring from mi - se - ry, That
36
we might live e - ter - nal - ly. Ky - ri - e -
Lord have
we might live e - ter - nal - ly. Ky - ri - e -
Lord have
we might live e - ter - nal - ly. Ky - ri - e -
Lord have
we might live e - ter - nal - ly. Ky - ri - e -
Lord have

41
pp
-lei - son. All this did he
mer - cy.
pp
-lei - son. All this did he
mer - cy.
pp
-lei - son. All this did he
mer - cy.
p cantabile
-lei - son. All this did he for
mer - cy.
47
f
for us free - ly, For to de - clare his great mer - cy; All
f
for us free - ly, For to de - clare his great mer - cy; All
f
for us free - ly, For to de - clare his great mer - cy; All
f
us free - ly, For to de - clare his great mer - cy; All
f

53
Christ - en - dom be mer - ry there - fore, And give him
Christ - en - dom be mer - ry there - fore, And give him
Christ - en - dom be mer - ry there - fore, And give him
Christ - en - dom be mer - ry there - fore, And give him
58
p
thanks for ev - er - more, ev - - - - er -
p
thanks for ev - er - more, ev - er - more.
p
thanks for ev - er - more. Ky - ri - e -
Lord have
p
thanks for ev - er - more. Ky - ri - e - lei -
Lord have mer -
p

63
-more. Ky - ri - e - lei - - - son, Ky - ri - e -
Lord have mer - - - cy, Lord have
Ky - ri - e - lei, e - lei - - - son, Ky - ri - e -
Lord have mer - cy, mer - - - cy, Lord have
-lei - - son, e - lei - - - son, Ky - ri - e -
mer - - cy, have mer - - - cy, Lord have
- son, Ky - ri - e - lei - - - son, Ky - ri - e -
- cy, Lord have mer - - - cy, Lord have
68
pp
- lei - - - - son.
mer - - - - cy.
pp
- lei - - - - son.
mer - - cy, mer - - - - cy.
pp
- lei - - - - son.
mer - - cy, mer - - - - cy.
pp
- lei - - - - son.
mer - - cy, mer - - - - cy.
pp

No sad thought his soul affright

from the cantata 'Hodie'

Verse 1: Anon.
Verse 2: Ursula Vaughan Williams (1911–2007)

RALPH VAUGHAN WILLIAMS (1872–1958)
piano arranged by John Leavitt

Duration: *c.*2.5 mins

This piece has been lowered a semitone from the original.

© Oxford University Press 1954 and 2020. Words reprinted by kind permission.

4
- fright, Sleep it is that mak - eth night; Let no
light, Stars and an - gels dance in flight; Joy of
- fright, Sleep it is that mak - eth night; Let no
light, Stars and an - gels dance in flight; Joy of
- fright, Sleep it is that mak - eth night; Let no
light, Stars and an - gels dance in flight; Joy of
- fright, Sleep it is that mak - eth night; Let
light, Stars and an - gels dance in flight; Joy
7
mur - mur nor rude wind To his slum - bers
heav'n shall now un - bind Chains of ev - il
mur - mur nor rude wind To his slum - bers
heav'n shall now un - bind Chains of ev - il
mur - mur nor rude wind To his slum - bers
heav'n shall now un - bind Chains of ev - il
no rude wind To his slum - bers
shall un - bind Chains of ev - il

10
ppp
prove un - kind: But a quire of an - gels
from man - kind, Love and joy their pow'r shall
ppp
prove un - kind: But a quire of an - gels
from man - kind, Love and joy their pow'r shall
ppp
prove un - kind: But a quire of an - gels
from man - kind, Love and joy their pow'r shall
ppp
prove un - kind: But a quire of an - gels
from man - kind, Love and joy their pow'r shall
13
make His dreams of heav'n, and let him wake To as
break, And for a new - born prin - ce's sake; Ne - ver
make His dreams of heav'n, and let him wake To as
break, And for a new - born prin - ce's sake; Ne - ver
make His dreams of heav'n, and let him wake To as
break, And for a new - born prin - ce's sake; Ne - ver
make His dreams of heav'n, and let him wake To as
break, And for a new - born prin - ce's sake; Ne - ver

16
ma - ny joys as can In this world be-fall a
since the world be - gan Such a light such dark did
ma - ny joys as can In this world be - fall a
since the world be - gan Such a light such dark did
ma - ny joys as can In this world be - fall a
since the world be - gan Such a light such dark did
ma - ny joys as can In this world be-fall a
since the world be - gan Such a light such dark did
19a
1.
2.
ppp
man. 2. Pro - mise span.
pp
Ped.

A Song of Thanksgiving

Song of the Three Holy Children, v. 29–31, 33
Henry V, Act IV, Scene 8
1 Chronicles 29: 11
Song of the Three Holy Children, v. 67

RALPH VAUGHAN WILLIAMS (1872–1958)
edited by John Leavitt

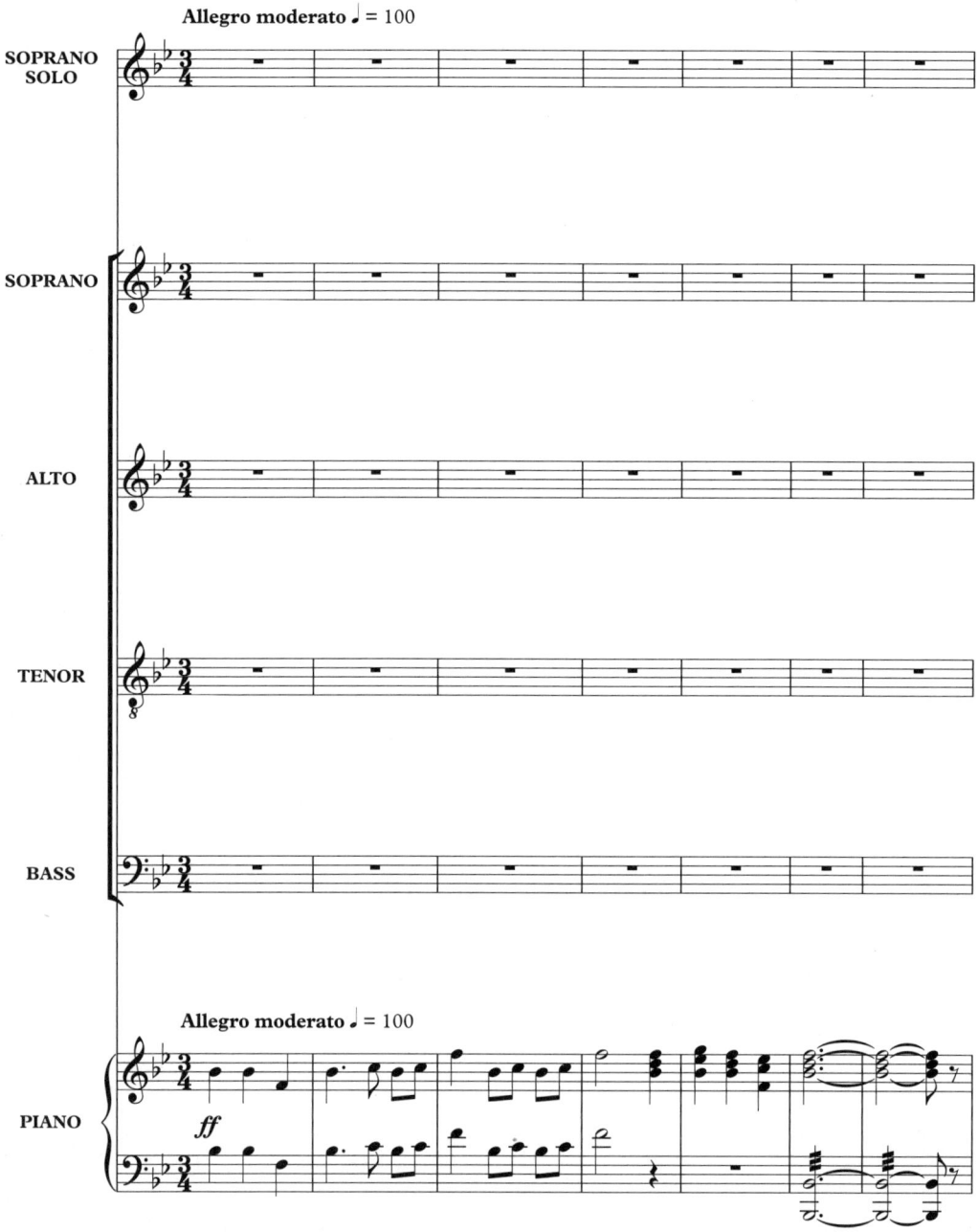

Duration: *c.*3.5 mins

© Oxford University Press 1945 and 2020

SOPRANO SOLO (or SOLI)
8
f
Bless-ed art thou, O Lord God of our fa - thers;
f
15
and to be praised and ex-alt - ed a - bove all for ev -
20
- er.
ff
25

31
(TUTTI) ff
S.
And bless-ed is thy glor-ious and ho-ly Name; and to be
A.
ff
And bless-ed is thy glor-ious and ho-ly Name; and to be
T.
ff
And bless-ed is thy glor-ious and ho-ly Name; and to be
B.
ff
And bless-ed is thy glor-ious and ho-ly Name; and to be
37
S. SOLO
f
Bless-ed art
S.
praised and glo-ri-fied a-bove all for ev-er.
A.
praised and glo-ri-fied a-bove all for ev-er.
T.
praised and glo-ri-fied a-bove all for ev-er.
B.
praised and glo-ri-fied a-bove all for ev-er.

42
S. SOLO
thou in the tem - ple of thine ho - ly glo - ry; and to be
p
47
S. SOLO
praised and ex - alt - ed a - bove all for ev - er.
S.
f
Bless - ed art thou on the glo -
A.
f
Bless - ed art thou on the glo -
T.
f
Bless - ed art thou on the glo -
B.
f
Bless - ed art thou on the glo -
f

52
S.
-rious throne of thy king - dom, and to be praised and
A.
-rious throne of thy king - dom, and to be praised and
to be
T.
-rious throne of thy king - dom, and to be praised and
B.
-rious throne of thy king - dom, and to be praised and
57
glo - ri-fied a - bove all for ev - er, for ev - er,
glo - ri-fied a - bove all for ev - er, for ev - er,
glo - ri-fied a - bove all for ev - er, for ev - er,
glo-ri - fied for ev - er, for ev - er, for ev - er,
Ped.

Speaker: the notation is purely conventional and does not imply any particular pitch, and need not be in absolute strict time, but must finish at the places where the piano and chorus swell up, through measure/bar 74.

67
not to us, but to thy arm a - lone a-scribe we all.
ev - er, for ev - - -
ev - er, for ev - er, for ev - -
ev - - er, for ev -
ev - er, for
pp

* This is only a 'safety' pause. If the speaker has already reached the last word then go on at once to the next bar.

75
(TUTTI) pp
S.
Thine, O Lord, is the great - ness, and the pow'r and the
pp
A.
Thine, O Lord, is the great - ness, and the pow'r and the
pp
T.
Thine, O Lord, is the great - ness, and the pow'r and the
pp
B.
Thine, O Lord, is the great - ness, and the pow'r and the
pp
81
cresc.
f
p
glo - ry. Thine is the vic - to - ry, and the ma - jes - ty; for
cresc.
f
p
glo - ry. Thine is the vic - to - ry, and the ma - jes - ty; for
cresc.
f
p
glo - ry. Thine is the vic - to - ry, and the ma - jes - ty; for
cresc.
f
p
glo - ry. Thine is the vic - to - ry, and the ma - jes - ty; for
cresc.
f
p

87
cresc.
f
all that is in the heav'n and earth is thine.
cresc.
f
all that is in the heav'n and earth is thine.
cresc.
f
all that is in the heav'n and earth is thine.
cresc.
f
all that is in the heav'n and earth is thine.
cresc.
f
92
ff
Thine is the king - dom, O Lord, and
ff
Thine is the king - dom, O Lord, and
ff
Thine is the king - dom, O Lord, and
ff
Thine is the king - dom, O Lord, and

98
thou art ex - alt - ed, Thou art ex -
thou art ex - alt - ed, Thou art ex -
thou art ex - alt - ed, Thou art ex -
thou art ex - alt - ed, Thou art ex -
ff
104
unis.
-alt - - ed, thou art ex - alt - ed as head
-alt - - ed, thou art ex - alt - - ed as head
-alt - - ed, thou art ex - alt - ed as head
-alt - ed, thou art ex - alt - ed as head

* Optional ending: for this final chord the left hand holds the same value as the right hand (see cue-sized note) and ends at the double bar, omitting the final vocal solo.

This is the truth

Trad. English

arr. by RALPH VAUGHAN WILLIAMS (1872–1958)
arr. for SATB choir and piano by John Leavitt

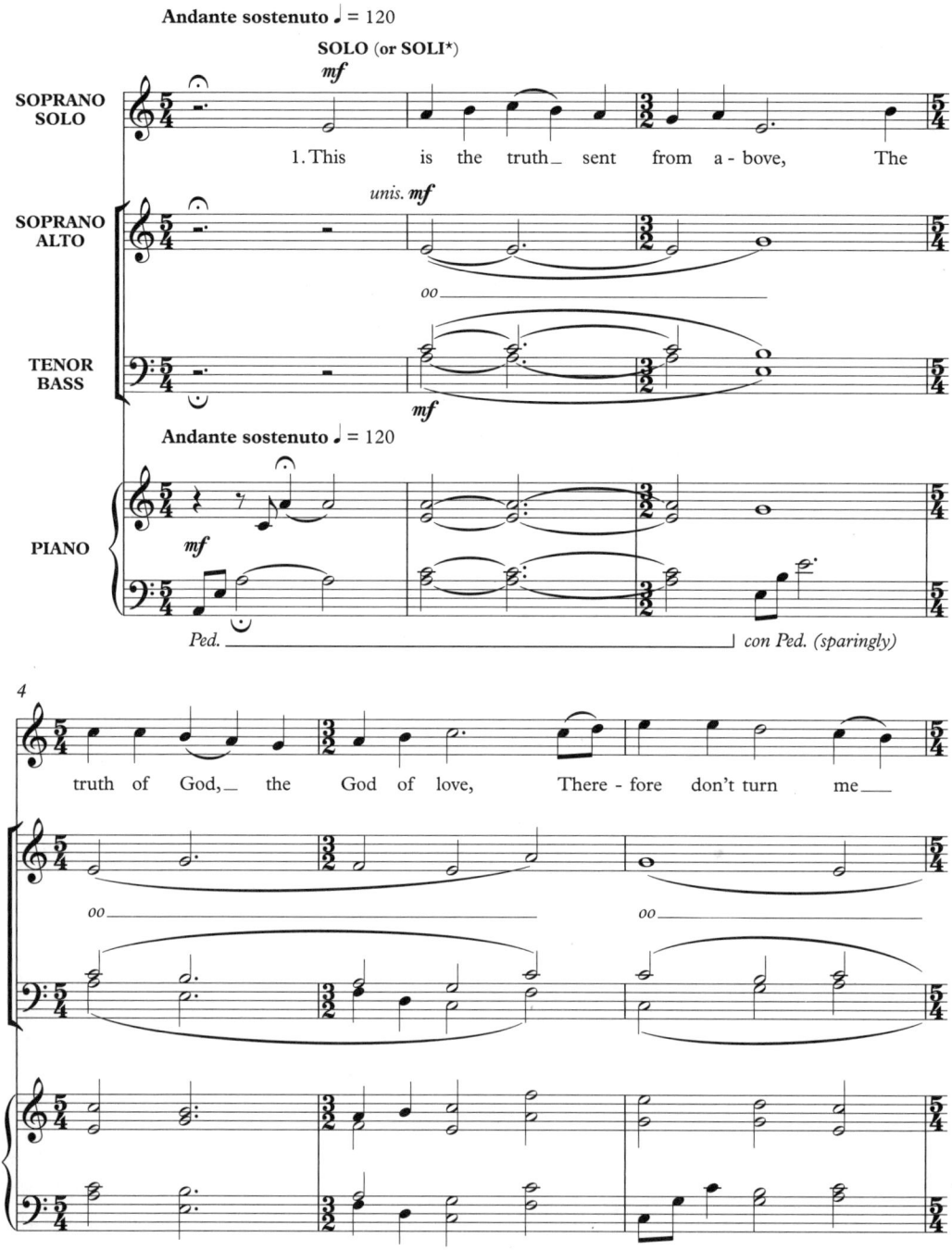

Duration: *c.*2 mins

* Sopranos sing in the absence of a soloist: either tutti or soli.

© Oxford University Press 1954 and 2020

7
from your door, But hearken all both rich and poor.
oo
2. The

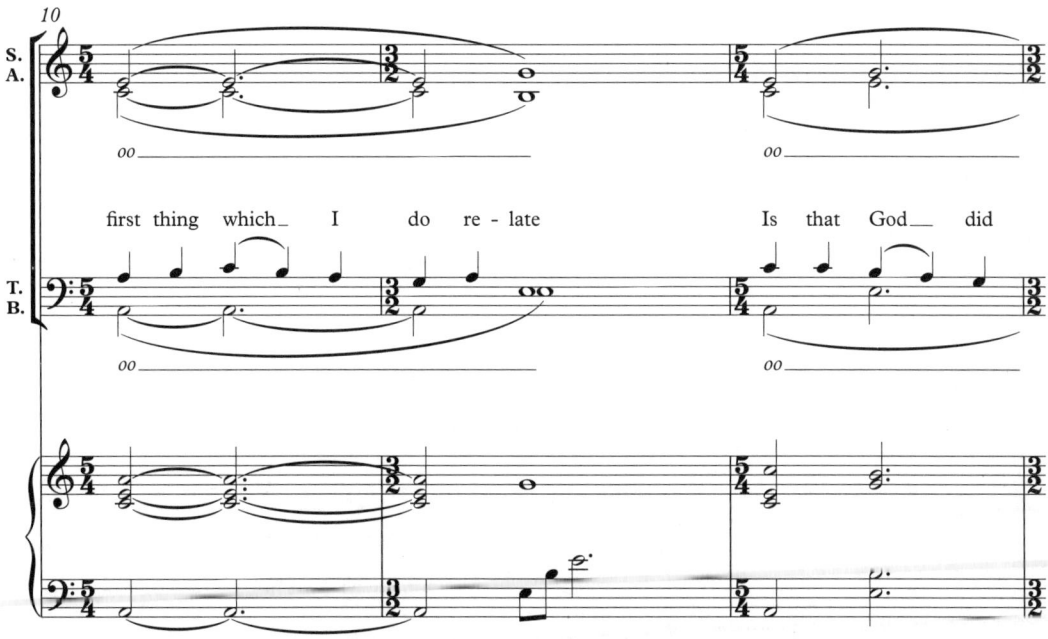
10
S.
A.
oo
oo
first thing which I do re - late
Is that God did
T.
B.
oo
oo

13
man cre - ate; The next thing which to you I'll tell Wo -
16
- man was made with man to dwell.
3. Thus
unis.
p
19
we were heirs to end - less woes, Till God the Lord did

22
in - ter - pose; And so a pro - mise soon did run That
25
he would re - deem us by his Son. 4. And at that sea - son
28
of the year Our blest Re - deem - er did ap - pear; He

31
here did live, and here did preach, And ma - ny thou - sands
34
DESCANT (OPT.)
f
5. Thus he to
S.
A.
unis. f
he did teach.
5. Thus he in love to
T.
B.
f
f

37
us be - haved, To show us
us be-haved, To show us how we must be saved; And
T.
B.

40
how we must be saved; Be pleased to hear
if you want to know the way, Be pleased to hear what he

43
what he did say, to hear
did say, to hear
45
S. SOLO
what he did say.
ff
S. A.
what he did say.
ff
T. B.
ff
ff

O taste and see

Psalm 34: 8

RALPH VAUGHAN WILLIAMS (1872–1958)
edited by John Leavitt

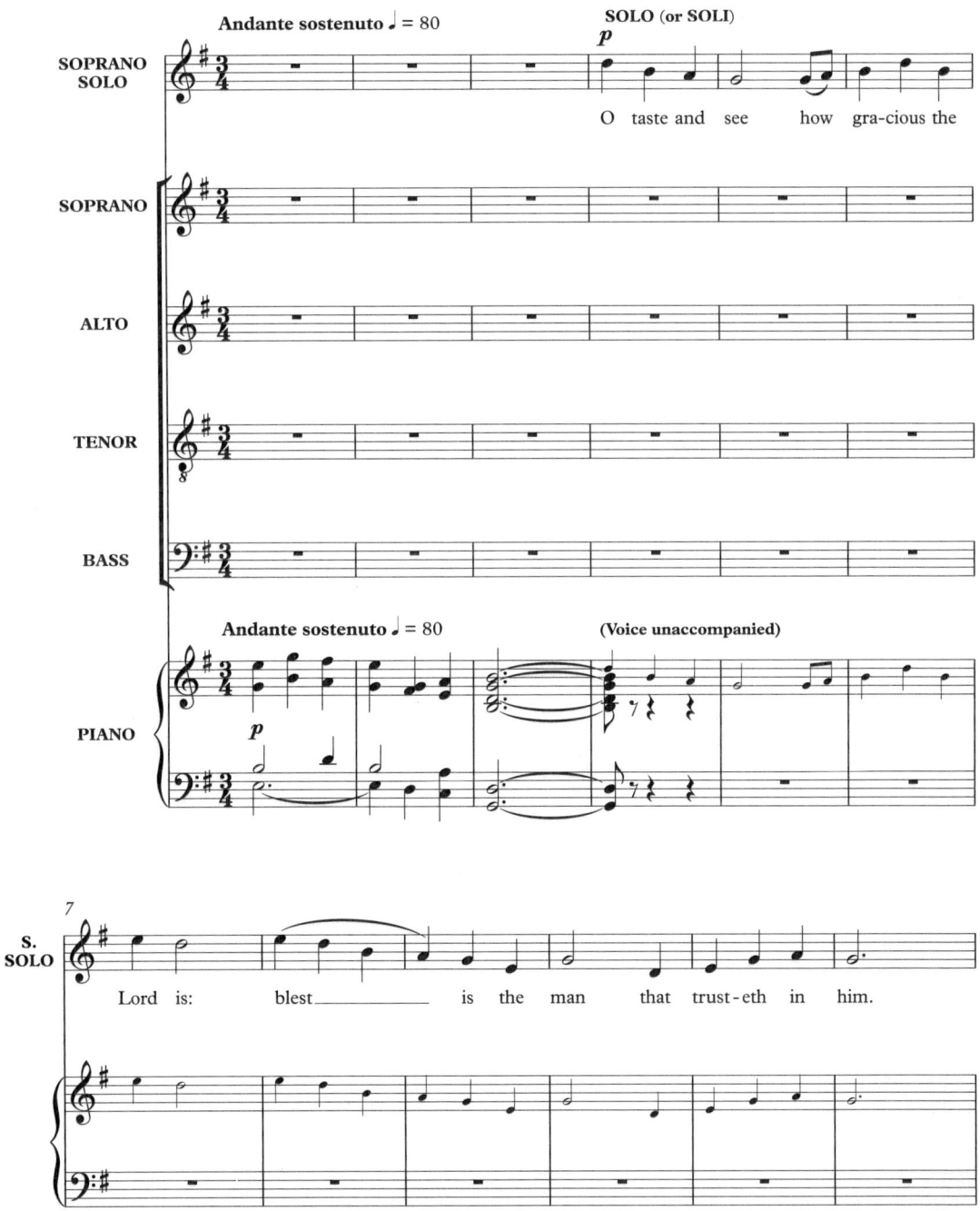

Duration: *c.*1 min

This motet may be sung in the key of G flat.

© Oxford University Press 1953 and 2020

* Optional: the voice parts may be doubled by the piano, if desired.

* Optional doubling of voices.

God rest you merry, gentlemen

Trad. English

arr. RALPH VAUGHAN WILLIAMS (1872–1958)
arr. for SATB choir by John Leavitt

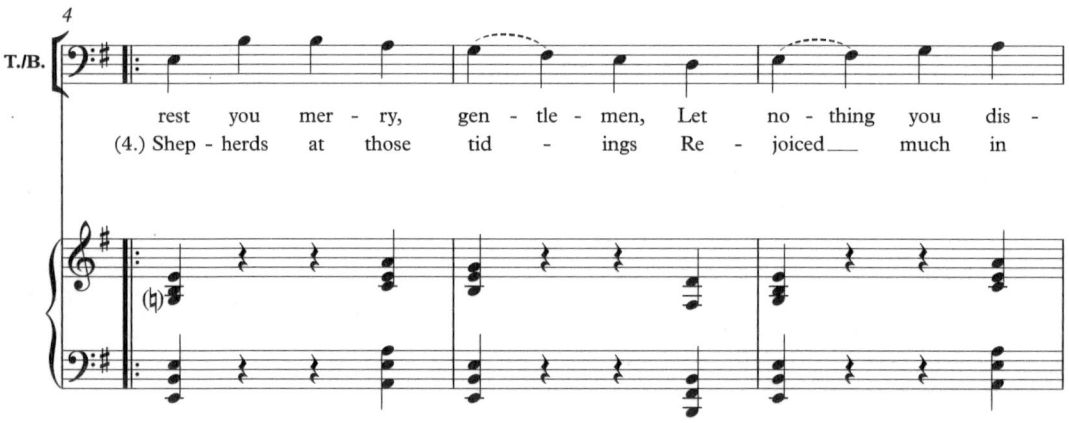

Duration: *c.*3 mins

© Oxford University Press 1954 and 2020

7
- may, Re - mem - ber Christ our Sa - viour was
mind, And left their flocks a - feed - ing In
10
born on Christ - mas Day, To save poor souls from
temp - est, storms of wind, And strait they came to
13
unis. f
S./A.
And it's
T./B.
Sa - tan's pow'r Which had long time gone a - stray,
f
Beth - le - hem, The Son of God to find.
f

16
tid - ings of com - fort and joy, com-fort and
19
S. p
A.
joy: And it's tid - ings of com - fort and joy.
2. In
5. Now
p
p
23
Beth - le - hem in Jew - ry this bless - ed babe was
when they came to Beth - le - hem, Where our sweet Sa - viour

26
born, And laid with - in a man - ger, Up -
lay, They found him in a man - ger Where
29
-on this bless - ed morn; The which his mo - ther
ox - en feed on hay, The bless - ed Vir - gin
T.
B.
32
unis.
f
Ma - ry No - thing did take in scorn:
kneel - ing down, Un - to the Lord did pray.
And it's
unis.
f
marcato
f

35
S.
A.
tid - - - - - - ings of joy, and it's
tid - ings of com - fort and joy, com-fort and joy, and it's
T.
B.
39
tid - - - ings of com - fort and
tid - ings of com - fort and joy.
42
joy.
(mf)
3. From God that is our Fa - ther the
6. Now to the Lord sing prai - ses, All
T.
B.
(mf)
(mf)

45
unis.
bless - ed Ang - els came, Un - to some cer - tain
you with - in this place, Like we true lov - ing
unis.
48
shep - herds with tid - ings of the same. That
Breth - ren, Each oth - er now em - brace, The
51
there was born in Beth - le - hem, The Son of God by
mer - ry time of Christ - mas Is draw - ing on a -

54
(ff)
name
- pace,
and it's tid - ings of com - fort and joy,
(ff)
ff
57
S.
A.
it's com - - fort and
it's com-fort and joy, and it's
tid - ings of
it's com - - fort and
T.
B.
it's com-fort and joy, and it's
1.
2.
com-fort and joy.
60a
com - fort and joy.
com - fort and joy.
(mf)
4. The
1.
2.
mf

Anthem for the dedication of a church or other festivals

O how amiable

Text from Psalms 84 and 90
and Isaac Watts (1674–1748)

RALPH VAUGHAN WILLIAMS (1872–1958)
arranged by John Leavitt

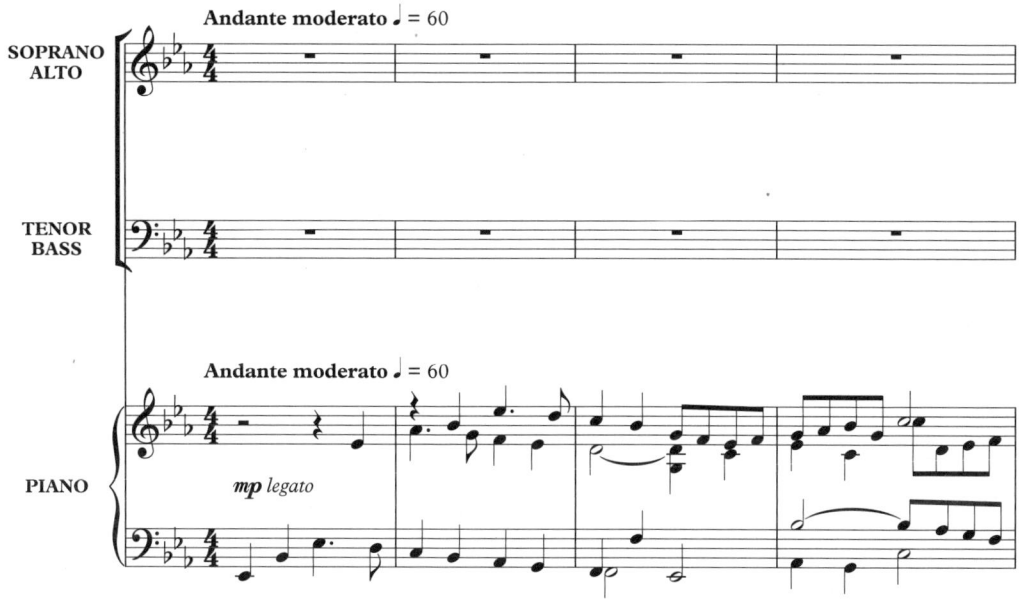

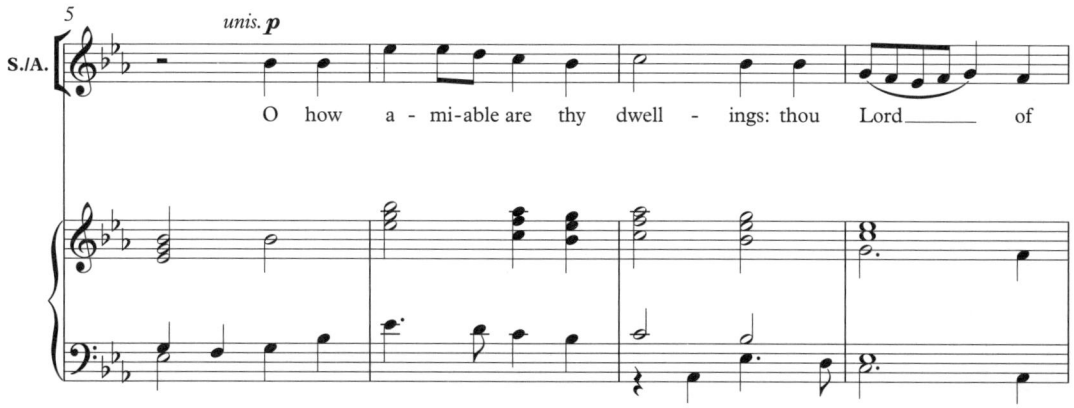

Duration: *c.*4 mins

© Oxford University Press 1940 and 2020

9
hosts! My soul hath a de-sire and
12
S./A.
long - ing to en - ter in - to the courts of the Lord: My
T./B.
unis. p
My heart and my
15
heart and my flesh re - joice in the liv - ing God.
flesh re - joice in the liv - ing God.

18
p
and the
p
Yea, the spar - row hath found her an house,
21
swal - low a nest where she may lay her young:
e - ven thy
p
24
f
S.
A.
al - tars, O Lord of hosts, my
T.
B.
f
f

27
S.
p
King and my God.
Bless - ed are they that
T.
p
Bless - ed are they that
p
30
S.
p
f
dwell in thy house:
A.
They will be al - way prais - ing
T.
dwell in thy house:
B.
p
f
f
33
Poco più mosso ♩ = 100
thee.
Poco più mosso ♩ = 100
f sostenuto

36
unis. ff
The glo - rious Ma-jes-ty of the
unis.
ff
39
Lord our God be up - on us: pros - per
42
thou the work of our hands up - on us.

45
unis.
O pros - per thou our han - dy-work,
unis.
49
O pros - per thou our han - dy - work.
54
ff

57
unis. ff
O God, our help in a - ges past, Our
unis.
ff
8vb
63
hope for years to come, Our shel - ter from the
69
ff
storm - y blast, And our e - ter - nal home.
ff
8vb

He that is down need fear no fall
(The woodcutter's song)

John Bunyan (1628–88)

RALPH VAUGHAN WILLIAMS (1872–1958)
arranged by John Leavitt

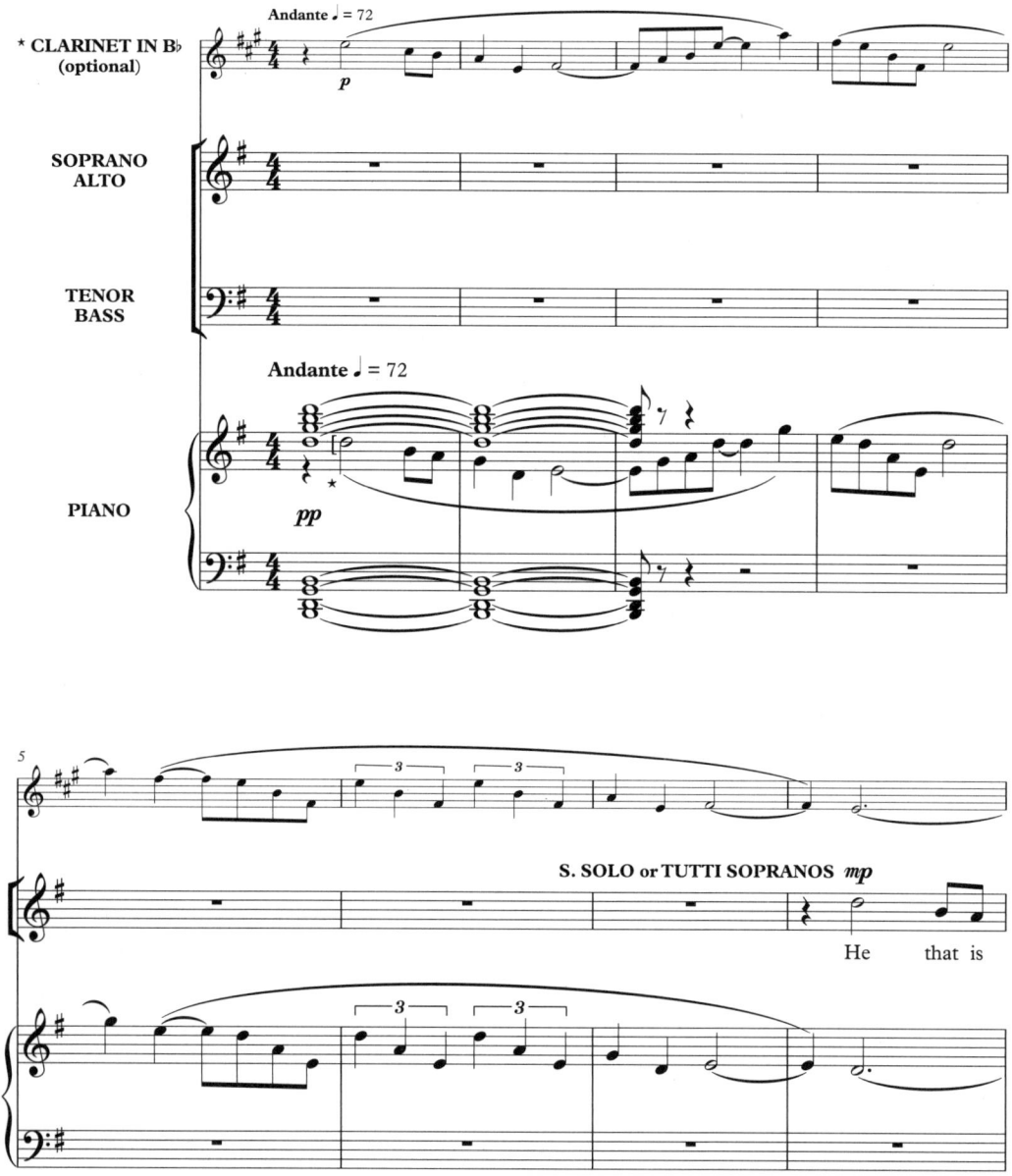

Duration: *c.*2.5 mins

* The passages between square brackets may be played by clarinet, flute, or recorder, in which case they should not be played on the piano.

This song was originally written for the stage-work *The Pilgrim's Progress*. It differs considerably from the present version, and is in the key of A flat.

© Oxford University Press 1950 and 2020

9
down need fear no fall; He that is low, no pride;
13
He that is hum-ble, ev - er shall Have God to be his Guide.
17
S.
A.
(TUTTI)
mp
I am con-
T.
B.
mp

21
-tent with what I have, Lit - tle be it or_ much; And, Lord, _con-
p legato

25
-tent - ment still I crave, Be - cause thou sav - est such.

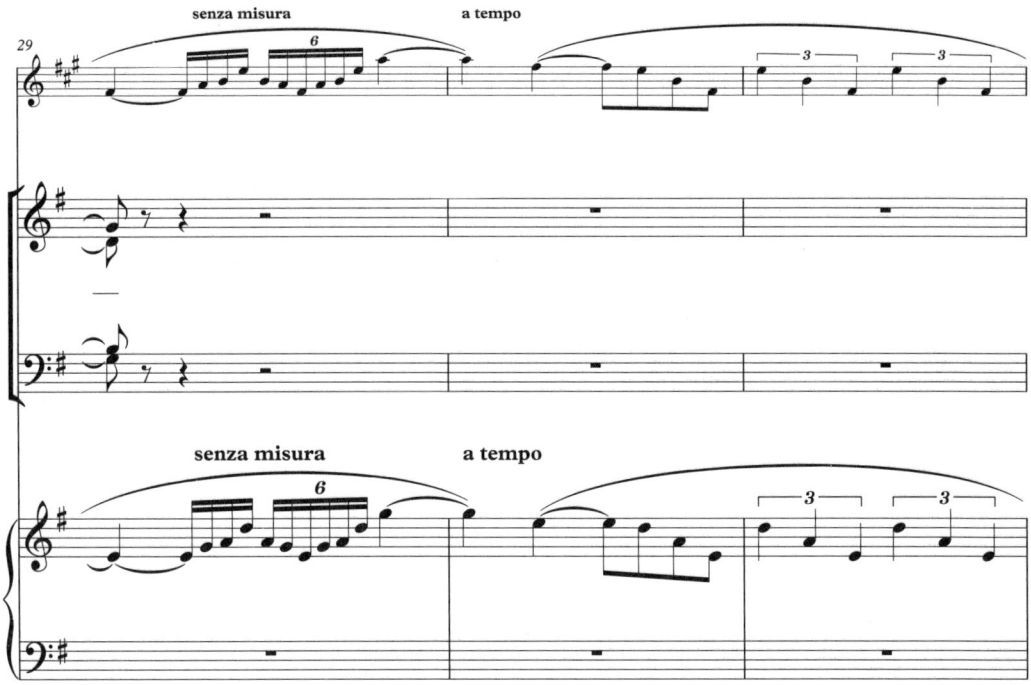
29
senza misura
a tempo
6
3
3
senza misura
a tempo
6
3
3

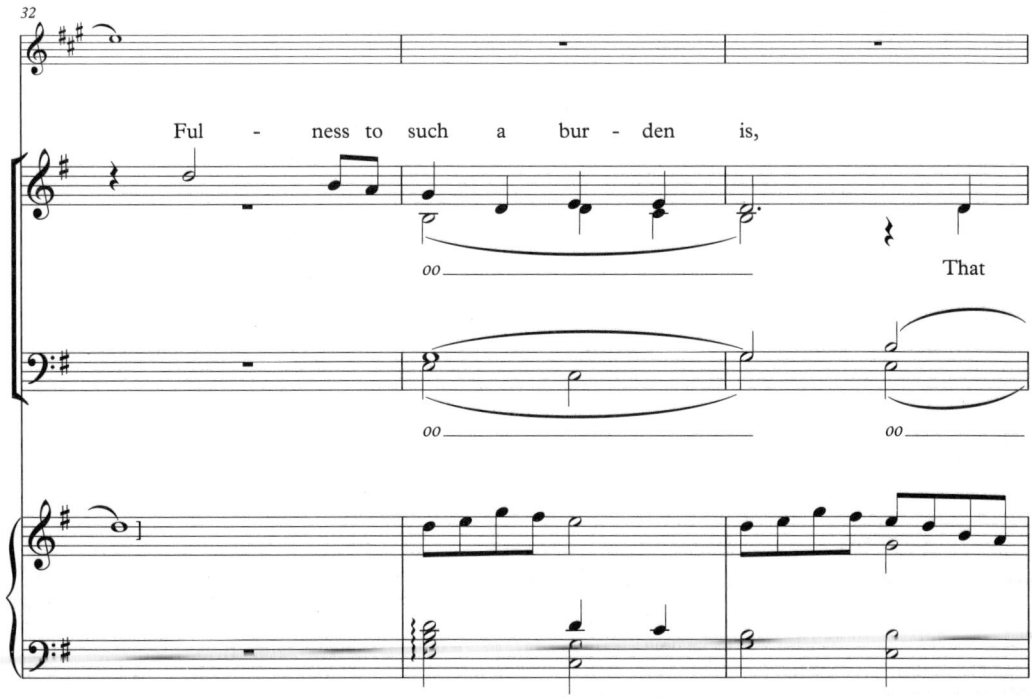
32
Ful - ness to such a bur - den is,
oo
That
oo
oo

35
go on pil - grim - age; Here lit - tle, and here - af - ter
Here lit - tle, and here - af - ter
38
Cl. (B♭)
S. A.
bliss, Is best from age to age.
T. B.
bliss, Is best from age to age.
41

At the name of Jesus

Caroline M. Noel (1817–77)

Tune: 'KING'S WESTON'
RALPH VAUGHAN WILLIAMS (1872–1958)
arranged by John Leavitt

Duration: *c.*11.5 mins

© Oxford University Press 1925, 1927, and 2020

8
Ev - 'ry tongue con - fess him King of glo - ry
All the An - gel fa - ces, All the hosts of
11
now; 'Tis the Fa - ther's plea - sure
light, Thrones and do - mi - na - tions,
14
We should call him Lord, Who from the be - gin - ning Was the
Stars up - on their way, All the heav'n-ly or - ders, In their

18
1.
2.
migh - ty Word.
great ar - - ray.
dim.
21
p
S.
A.
3. Hum-bled for a sea - - son, To re - ceive a
T.
B.
24
name From the lips of sin - - ners

27
Un - to whom he came, Faith - ful - ly he
30
cresc.
bore it Spot - less to the last,
cresc.
cresc.
33
f
S.
Brought it back vic - to - rious When from death
f
A.
Brought it back vic - to - rious When from death he
T.
B.
f
f
f

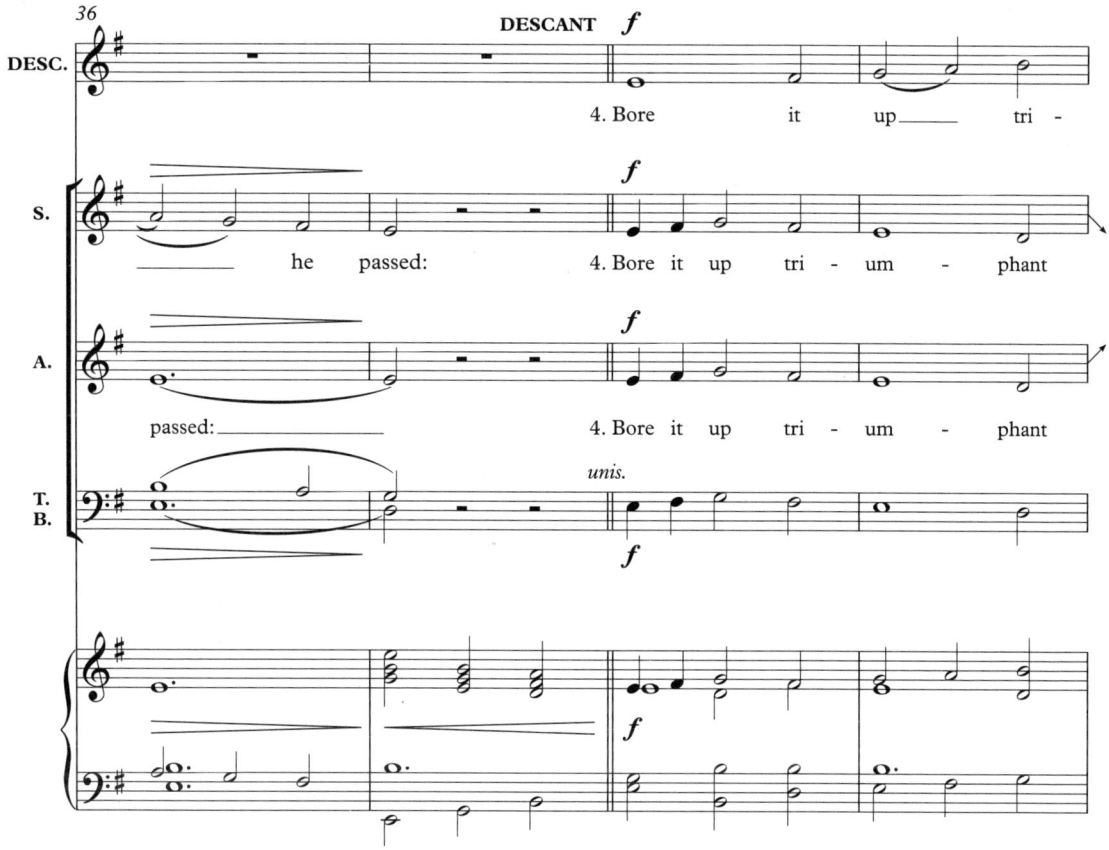
36
DESCANT
f
DESC.
4. Bore it up tri -
S.
he passed: 4. Bore it up tri - um - phant
A.
passed: 4. Bore it up tri - um - phant
unis.
T.
B.

40
DESC.
- um - - phant With its hu - - man
unis.
S.
A.
With its hu - man light, Through all ranks of
T.
B.

43
light, Through all ranks of
crea - tures, To the cen - tral height,

46
crea - tures, To the cen - - - tral
To the throne of God - head, To the Fa - ther's breast;

50
height, Filled it with the glo - - -
Filled it with the glo - ry Of that per - - fect

53
- ry Of that per - fect rest.
rest.

57
pp
S.
A.
5. Name him, bro - thers, name him, With love as strong as
T.
B.
pp
pp
60
death, But with awe and won - der,
63
cresc.
And with ba - ted breath; He is God the
cresc.
cresc.

66
Sa - - viour, He is Christ the Lord,
69
dim.
Ev - er to be wor - shipped, Trust-ed and a -
dim.
dim.
72
DESCANT mf
DESC.
6. In your hearts en -
p
unis. mf
S.
A.
- dored.
6. In your hearts en - throne him;
unis.
T.
B.
p
mf
p
mf

76
-throne him; There let him sub - due
There let him sub - due All that is not ho - ly,

80
All that is not ho - - - - ly,
All that is not true: Crown him as your cap - tain

84
cresc.
All that is not true: Let his
cresc.
In temp - ta - tion's hour; Let his will en -
cresc.
87
will en - fold you in its
- fold you In its light and pow'r.

90
light and pow'r.
cresc.
94
ff
S.
A.
7. Bro - thers, this Lord Je - - sus Shall re - turn a -
T.
B.
ff
ff
97
- gain, With his Fa - ther's glo - ry,

100
With his An - gel train; For all wreaths of
103
em - - pire Meet up - on his brow,
106
And our hearts con - fess him King of glo - ry now.

Let us now praise famous men

Ecclesiasticus 44

RALPH VAUGHAN WILLIAMS (1872–1958)
arranged for SATB choir by John Leavitt

Duration: *c.*2 mins

© 1923 Chester Music Limited trading as J Curwen and Sons. Chester Music Limited. This arrangement © 2020 Chester Music Limited trading as J Curwen and Sons. All rights reserved. International copyright secured. Used by permission of Hal Leonard Europe Limited.

13
Lead - ers of the peo - ple by their coun - sels, and by_ their
17
know - ledge.
unis. p
Such as found out mu - si - cal tunes, and re -
subito p
22
unis. f
All these were ho-noured in their
-cit - ed ver - ses in writ - ing:
unis.
f
cresc.
f

26
largamente
a tempo
ff
gen - er - a - tions, and were the glo - ry of their times.
ff
largamente
a tempo
ff
30
unis. pp
And some there be, which have no me - mo - ri -
TENORS
pp
subito pp
34
- al; who are per-ished, as though they had ne - ver been.

38
Their bo - dies are bu - ried in peace;
T.
B.
pp
42
unis. cresc.
f
cresc.
but their name liv - eth for ev - - er -
unis.
cresc.
f
cresc.
cresc.
f
45
ff
- more.
ff
ff

He that is down need fear no fall
(The woodcutter's song)

RALPH VAUGHAN WILLIAMS (1872–1958)
arranged by John Leavitt

© Oxford University Press 1950 and 2020